PEOPLE & PLACES

By Moira Butterfield
Illustrated by Chris Forsey

RANDOM HOUSE NEW YORK

First American edition, 1991

Library of Congress Cataloging-in-Publication Data
Butterfield, Moira.
People & places / by Moira Butterfield;
illustrated by Chris Forsey.
p. cm.—(A Random House tell me about book)
Includes index.
Summary: Question and answer format is used to explore
the diversity of races, ethnic groups, nationalities,
and cultures of humankind in many settings around the world.
Includes suggestions for projects and activities.
ISBN 0–679–80868–X
1. Ethnology—Juvenile literature.
2. Human geography—Juvenile literature.
[1. Ethnology. 2. Manners and customs.
3. Handicraft. 4. Questions and answers.]
I. Forsey, Christopher, ill.
II. Title.
III. Title: People and places.
IV. Series.
GN333.B87 1991b
305.8—dc20
91–214

Manufactured in Spain 1 2 3 4 5 6 7 8 9 10

Contents

How many people are there?

There are about 5 billion people living in the world today. The number of people who live in a particular place or area is known as its population. For thousands of years the world's population increased slowly. But over the past 200 years there has been a population explosion and the number of people living in the world has increased dramatically. If this continues, there will be nearly three times as many people in 60 years' time!

POPULATION FACTS

● Over 200,000 people are born every day—that's about 140 babies a minute!

● Currently, one person in three is under the age of 15.

● The country with the biggest population is China. About one billion people live there—one fifth of the world's population.

● Japanese people tend to live longest. On average, they live for nearly 75 years.

1 In 8000 B.C. there were about 6 million people in the world. Most people lived on the continents of Asia and Africa.

DO YOU KNOW

Human beings have only been around for a tiny fraction of the Earth's existence.
   Imagine that the Earth was formed exactly one year ago—on January 1. That would mean that our earliest ancestors did not appear until the afternoon of December 31!

2 By A.D. 1, the world's population had grown to about 138 million people. People now lived in most parts of the world.

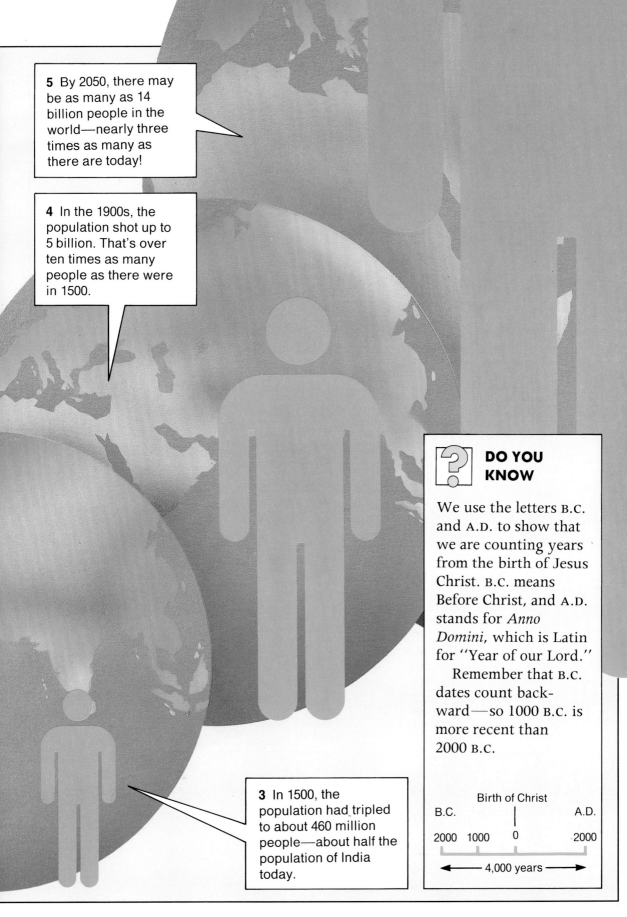

5 By 2050, there may be as many as 14 billion people in the world—nearly three times as many as there are today!

4 In the 1900s, the population shot up to 5 billion. That's over ten times as many people as there were in 1500.

3 In 1500, the population had tripled to about 460 million people—about half the population of India today.

DO YOU KNOW

We use the letters B.C. and A.D. to show that we are counting years from the birth of Jesus Christ. B.C. means Before Christ, and A.D. stands for *Anno Domini*, which is Latin for "Year of our Lord."

Remember that B.C. dates count backward—so 1000 B.C. is more recent than 2000 B.C.

```
                    Birth of Christ
                          |
   B.C.                   |              A.D.

   2000    1000           0              2000
   |_____|_____|_____|
        ←——— 4,000 years ———→
```

What is a country?

A country is an area of land that belongs to a group of people who share laws by which they live. The people who live in a country are known as its nation. A country is usually run by members of its own nation who make up its government. Such countries are called independent and have their own national anthem, or song, and a flag. There are about 170 independent countries today.

KEY TO MAP

1	Albania	34	Haiti	65	San Marino
2	Andorra	35	Honduras	66	Senegal
3	Austria	36	Hungary	67	Sierra Leone
4	Bahrain	37	Iceland	68	Singapore
5	Bangladesh	38	Ireland	69	Sri Lanka
6	Belgium	39	Jamaica	70	Surinam
7	Belize	40	Jordan	71	Swaziland
8	Benin	41	Kampuchea (Cambodia)	72	Switzerland
9	Bhutan			73	Taiwan
10	Brunei	42	Korea, North	74	Thailand
11	Bulgaria	43	Korea, South	75	Togo
12	Burkina Faso	44	Kuwait	76	Trinidad and Tobago
13	Burundi	45	Lesotho		
14	Central African Republic	46	Liberia	77	Tunisia
		47	Liechtenstein	78	United Arab Emirates
15	Costa Rica	48	Luxembourg		
16	Cuba	49	Malawi	79	Uruguay
17	Cyprus	50	Malta	80	Vatican City
18	Czechoslovakia	51	Monaco	81	Vietnam
19	Denmark	52	Netherlands	82	Yugoslavia
20	Djibouti	53	New Zealand	83	Zimbabwe
21	Dominica	54	Nicaragua		
22	Dominican Republic	55	Panama		
23	Ecuador	56	Papua New Guinea		
24	El Salvador	57	Philippines		
25	Equatorial Guinea	58	Portugal		
26	Gambia	59	Qatar		
27	Germany	60	Romania		
28	Ghana	61	Rwanda		
29	Great Britain	62	St. Christopher and Nevis		
30	Greece				
31	Guatemala	63	St. Lucia		
32	Guinea-Bissau	64	St. Vincent and the Grenadines		
33	Guyana				

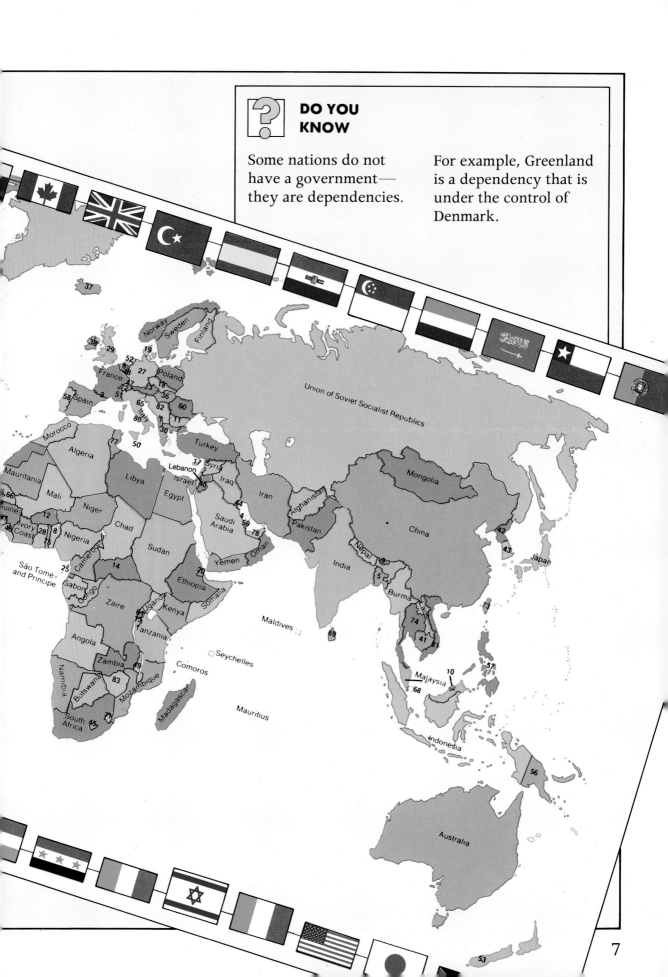

DO YOU KNOW

Some nations do not have a government— they are dependencies.

For example, Greenland is a dependency that is under the control of Denmark.

37

Norway
Sweden
Finland

36
29
19
52
58
27
France
47
18 Poland
58 Spain
2 5
3
36
65
82 60
Italy 11
80
30
77 50
Turkey
Morocco
Algeria
17 Syria
Lebanon
Israel
Iraq
46
Mauritania
Libya
Egypt
Iran
Afghanistan
Mongolia
6 66
Mali
Niger
44
China
42
Guinea
12
Saudi
Arabia
4
Pakistan
43
46 Ivory
Coast
28 8
Nigeria
59 78
Japan
16
Chad
Sudan
Yemen Oman
Nepal
India
9
São Tomé
and Principe
25 Cameroon
14
Gabon
Ethiopia
20
5
Congo
Zaire
Uganda
61
Kenya
Somalia
Burma
73
13
Angola
Tanzania
74
Maldives
69
41 61
Zambia
49
Seychelles
Comoros
10
Namibia
83
Mozambique
Malaysia
57
Botswana
68
South
Africa 45
70
Madagascar
Mauritius
Indonesia
56

Union of Soviet Socialist Republics

Australia

53

7

What is the world's biggest country?

The U.S.S.R. is the biggest country in the world. It covers nearly one-seventh of the Earth's land area, and it is so large that when it is nighttime in some parts of the country, other parts are still in daylight! Because of its size, this vast country has many different kinds of climate and countryside.

U.S.S.R. FACTS

● It would take over two years to walk around the borders of the U.S.S.R. — a journey of 66,000 miles.

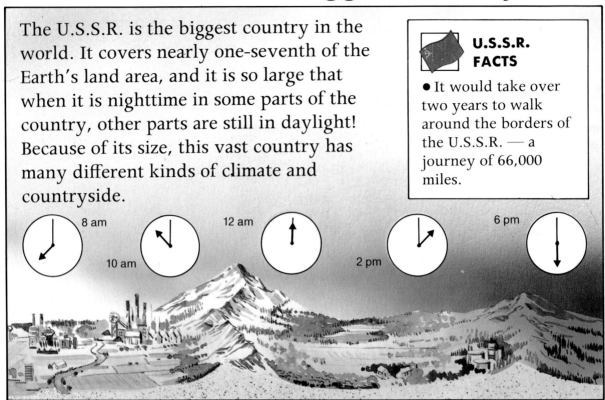

What is the world's smallest country?

The smallest independent country is the State of the Vatican City in the Italian city of Rome. It covers an area of 108 acres— about the size of an average city park. It is the headquarters of the Roman Catholic Church and has a population of just 1,000 people.

DO YOU KNOW

The Vatican City has its own flag, radio station, and railroad. It even issues its own stamps!

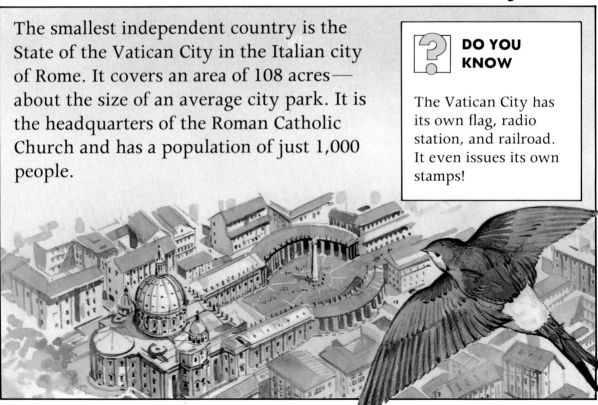

What is the most visited country?

The country with the highest number of visitors is Spain, which has about 42 million tourists every year. It is followed by France, then the U.S.A., Italy, Austria, the United Kingdom, and Canada. The number of tourists throughout the world is growing fast, as more and more people decide to go abroad for their vacations.

DO YOU KNOW

When visiting another country, you usually have to show your passport. This is a document that says who you are, what you look like, and what country you are from. The word *passport* comes from documents used for ships visiting ports.

The most popular tourist spots in Spain are the magnificent beaches along its Mediterranean coast.

France is the second-most visited country. Its most famous sight is the spectacular Eiffel Tower in Paris.

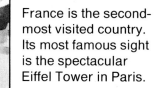

The U.S.A. has 23 million visitors a year. The Statue of Liberty, in New York harbor, is a popular attraction.

Italy is visited by 20 million people a year. The Colosseum in Rome is one of the world's best-known tourist spots.

MAKE A POSTER

Find out more about your area by making a big tourist poster. List some interesting sites to visit and things to do. Add some photos, postcards, or pictures cut from magazines to show the places that you think tourists should visit.

Unlike other tourist countries, Austria is busiest in the winter, during the ski season.

How many languages are there?

Nearly 5,000 languages are spoken around the world, but many are used only by small groups of people. In India, for example, there are 16 main languages and 1,000 minor ones which are only spoken in certain parts of the country.

These children are all saying "hello." The words are written as they sound, rather than as they're spelled.

DO YOU KNOW

The sun is in the sky.

The master is in the house.

JAM-BO

Swahili is spoken all over the east coast of Africa.

MAR-HU-BA

Many forms of Arabic are spoken throughout the Middle East.

KON-NEE-CHEE-WA

Japanese is spoken by the 124 million people of Japan.

The first written languages used picture symbols instead of an alphabet made up of different letters. One of the earliest symbol languages was developed in Egypt about 5,000 years ago. These ancient symbols are called hieroglyphics.

Two hieroglyphic sentences are shown in the picture above.

BWEN-OS DEE-OS

Spanish is spoken in Spain, Central America, and South America.

ESPANA

NAM-AS-TAY

Hindi is spoken by a third of the people in India.

Which language do most people speak?

The language with the largest number of speakers is Mandarin. It is the main language of China and it is spoken by over 715 million people.

Unlike English, Mandarin has no alphabet. Instead, it uses about 50,000 picture symbols called characters. Some words are formed by simple characters which are easy to understand. Other words are made up of two or more characters mixed together. One of the most complicated words is ''talkative''—it contains 64 characters!

MAN SKY

Characters must be drawn with great care. Often there is only a tiny difference between one character and another with a different meaning.

11

What is a government?

A government is a group of people who run a country—*govern* means "run" or "rule." Governments are responsible for all sorts of things, from making new laws to collecting taxes and deciding how they should be spent. People involved in running the country are called politicians, and the work they do is known as politics.

DO YOU KNOW

At the United Nations, governments come together to talk about world issues. The UN flag shows the world surrounded by laurel leaves, which are symbols of peace.

The members of the government with the most important jobs are often called the cabinet.

In most countries, one person is chosen to head the government—as president or prime minister, for example.

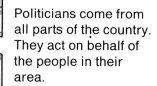

Politicians come from all parts of the country. They act on behalf of the people in their area.

 GOVERNMENT FACTS

• In many countries, the people vote to elect, or choose, their government. This system is called a democracy. Voting takes place every few years, in elections.

• A country headed by a king or queen is called a monarchy.

• Some countries are ruled by one person called a dictator.

• Communist countries are ruled by one very powerful group of politicians called the Communist party.

The Roman emperor Julius Caesar was a dictator.

What is a parliament?

A parliament is a body of people responsible for making a country's laws. One of the oldest parliaments is in the United Kingdom. It is made up of two houses, or parts. One house is for elected politicians, and the other is for nobles and churchmen.

The UK parliament meets in the Houses of Parliament on the bank of the Thames River in London. The famous old clock below is called Big Ben, although Big Ben is really the great bell that rings out the hours.

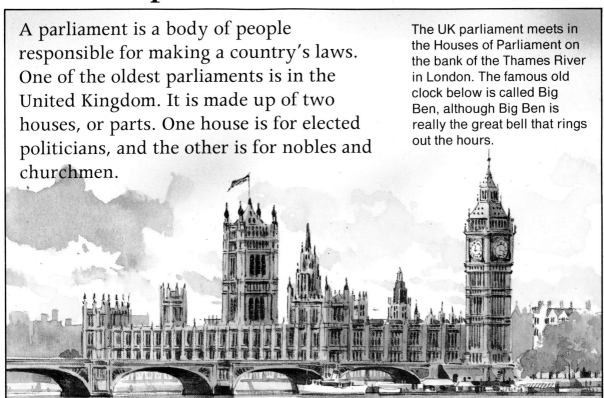

What are taxes?

Taxes are sums of money collected from the people by governments. They are needed to pay for services we all use, such as the police, the armed forces, education, and some health care.

Many countries have a free national health service, which anybody can use. This is paid for with money raised by taxes.

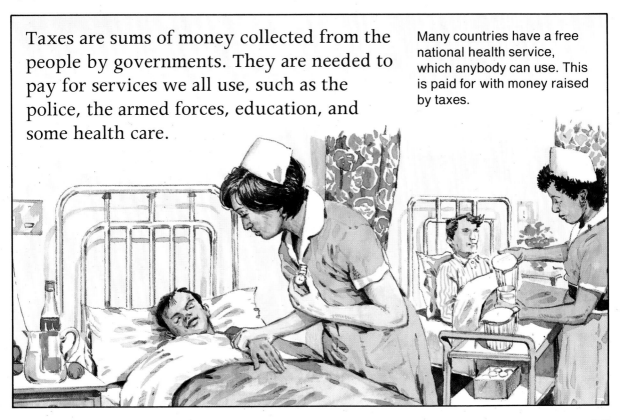

What are the main religions?

The three largest religions in the world are Christianity, Islam, and Hinduism. But there are several other major religions and thousands of smaller ones.

Each religion has its own beliefs and methods of worship. Some people believe there is just one god; others believe there are many. Most religions have special ceremonies which are performed inside holy buildings called temples or churches.

Christianity was started nearly 2,000 years ago by the followers of Jesus Christ. Christians believe in one god and in the teachings of a book called the Bible.

Hinduism is the main religion of India and other countries nearby. Its followers believe in many gods, but the most important ones are Brahma, Vishnu, and Shiva.

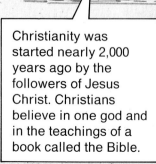

RELIGION FACTS

● Followers of the Indian religion Jainism try to avoid harming any living creature.

● Christianity is followed by about a third of the world's population. Islam is second, with about a fifth of the world's population.

● The largest temple ever built is Angkor Wat (City Temple) in Cambodia. It takes about five hours to walk from one end to the other.

The followers of Judaism are called Jews. The religion was founded by Abraham in about 1900 B.C. Jews believe in one god, and their holy book is the Hebrew Bible.

Islam was founded in Arabia by Muhammad in A.D. 622. Followers of the religion are called Muslims. They believe that there is one god, and their holy book is the Koran.

Buddhism is based on the teachings of Siddhartha Gautama, an Indian prince who lived over 2,500 years ago. Great teachers of this religion are given the title ''Buddha.''

15

What is Mardi Gras?

Mardi Gras is a festival that takes place in many countries every year on Shrove Tuesday. This is the last day before the time of year known as Lent, when Christians traditionally fast, or go without fat and meat. Mardi Gras is French for "fat Tuesday."

During Mardi Gras, crowds of people wearing fancy dress parade through the streets and dance to the music of marching bands.

FESTIVAL FACTS

● The word *festival* means "feast day."

● The Romans spent over 100 days a year feasting in honor of their gods.

● Dozens of countries around the world hold festivals on their Independence Day— to celebrate the time when they gained their freedom from foreign control.

MAKE A CARNIVAL MASK

Here's a way to make a carnival mask from cardboard and yarn.

1 With an adult's help, cut an oval shape out of thin cardboard. Make holes for the eyes and mouth.

2 Paint on a face using brightly colored pens. Stick colored yarn or paper strips around the top to make hair.

3 Make a hole in each side of the mask, then thread a piece of yarn through each hole and fix it with a knot.

When is Chinese New Year?

The Chinese New Year begins on the first full moon between January 21 and February 19. The celebrations last for two weeks and begin with visits to friends and relatives. On the last day, big street parades are often held.

DO YOU KNOW

Chinese New Year parades are usually headed by a giant dragon. It weaves through the streets to the noise of gongs and firecrackers, keeping away evil spirits.

Who is Santa Claus?

The name Santa Claus comes from Saint Nicholas, a Christian bishop who lived over 1,500 years ago. These days the saint is remembered in many countries as Santa Claus or Father Christmas.

Santa Claus is well known as the kindly old gentleman who brings children presents at Christmas.

Why do people wear different clothes?

People wear different clothes for different purposes—such as for work or leisure, or for protection against the weather. Some clothes are worn only on special occasions, and others simply because they are fashionable.

? DO YOU KNOW

The word *jeans* comes from Genoa, the Italian town which used to produce the tough canvas material they are made from.

Desert people's robes are ideal for keeping off the hot sun during the day and for providing warmth during the cold nights.

The Amish people in the U.S.A. have religious reasons for wearing simple black clothes designed in the style of the 1800s.

Women in Brittany, in France, wear traditional clothes at festival times. Their tall lace headdresses are called *coiffes*.

Some people wear uniforms to show what their job is. This uniform is worn by Canada's Royal Mounted Police.

CLOTHES FACTS

● At $2 million each, the U.S. shuttle astronauts' spacesuits are the most expensive clothes ever made.

● The zipper was invented last century, but it took 50 years to produce a version that didn't pop open.

● The most expensive fabric is vicuna, at over $8,000 a yard.

In Japan, the kimono first made its appearance over 1,000 years ago. It is still sometimes worn by both men and women.

In many countries, everyday dress depends on fashion. The clothes that are in fashion change all the time.

DESIGN A COSTUME

Do you know what your country's national costume looks like? Try designing your own version, basing it on a mixture of old and new styles of clothing.

When were the first theaters built?

No one knows when people first started acting and making up plays, but we do know that the first theaters were built by the ancient Greeks about 7,000 years ago. Greek plays developed from a yearly festival worshiping a god named Dionysus. During the celebrations, tales of gods and heroes were told in songs and dances.

 DO YOU KNOW

The first Greek plays were called tragedies, from the Greek words for "goat song." Goats were sacrificed during the plays.

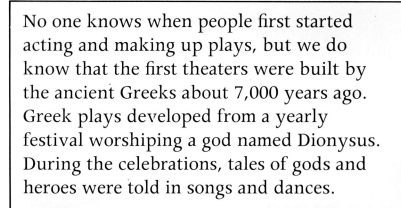

Hardly any objects were used to show where each scene was taking place. The audience relied on the actors to describe the location.

Actors changed their costumes inside a *skene*. Paintings hanging outside were used to show where the play was set.

The chorus danced and sang in the circular area called the orchestra. Their role was to comment on the play.

 DO YOU KNOW

Kabuki is a spectacular form of Japanese drama. The actors wear colorful costumes, and the story is told through a mixture of words, songs, and mime.

The audience sat in rows of seats built into a sloping hillside. The largest theaters could hold up to 17,000 people.

Why do we play music?

Music has always been important to us because it affects our emotions. It can make us feel relaxed or excited, happy or sad. Even if you can't play a musical instrument, you can still have great fun by singing or dancing to music.

DO YOU KNOW

The earliest music was played to keep gods and spirits happy. Some tribes in remote places still use music for the same reason.

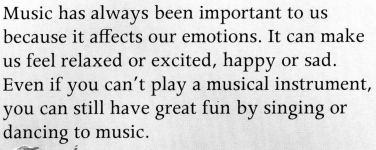

Most modern music relies on electronic instruments such as the electric guitar.

The violin has been one of the most widely used musical instruments for 500 years.

The didgeridoo has been played by Australian Aborigines for thousands of years.

When did painting begin?

The earliest paintings ever found were done 27,000 years ago on cave walls in France. They show pictures of wild animals such as bison, deer, and horses. The painters might have been trying to work magic to improve their hunting.

DO YOU KNOW

The world's most valuable painting is the *Mona Lisa* by Leonardo da Vinci. It's not for sale, but it's insured for over $100 million.

Cave dwellers made their paints from plants, berries, earth, and pieces of charcoal, or burned wood. They mixed the materials together to create colors.

What is the oldest sport?

The oldest sport of all is wrestling, which goes back at least 4,500 years. The sport is still very popular all over the world. In Japan, sumo wrestlers are national heroes, and huge crowds go to see their matches.

SPORTS FACTS

• Tennis began as an indoor game played by French noblemen 800 years ago.

• Baseball developed from a centuries-old English bat and ball game called rounders.

• Basketball was invented by an American gym teacher in 1891 to make his classes more lively.

Sumo wrestlers try to force their opponents to the ground or out of the ring.

When were the first Olympic Games?

The first Olympic Games were held at Olympus in Greece nearly 3,000 years ago. After 1,000 years, the tradition of holding games every four years died out. It was not revived until 1896—after a gap of 1,500 years.

DO YOU KNOW

Before each Olympics, a special torch is lit at Olympus. It is held in front of a mirror until it is lit by the heat of the sun. The torch is then carried by runners all the way to the city where the Games are being held. The final runner enters the stadium and lights a flame that burns throughout the Games.

During the Games, there are usually several events going on at the same time.

What is the most popular sport?

Soccer is the most popular sport of all. It is played and watched by millions of people everywhere. Many countries have several big soccer clubs, whose teams regularly play against each other. The top players can earn large sums of money.

SOCCER FACTS

● One version of soccer played 700 years ago involved hundreds of players in each team. Games were played between towns, with the goals up to a mile apart.

● The world's longest soccer match lasted 3 hours, 30 minutes. It was a tie, held in Brazil.

● The match with the most goals was between two Yugoslavian teams. The score was 134–1!

Brazil and Italy have both won the World Cup three times. Brazil has appeared in every competition since it began in 1930.

At the end of the competition the winning team is presented with a magnificent trophy made of solid gold.

More than a billion people watch the World Cup—in soccer stadiums and on television all around the world.

The World Cup is held every four years. Over 100 national soccer teams take part in the early rounds.

How many different jobs are there?

There are thousands and thousands of different jobs. In the United States, the Department of Labor puts the figure at about 20,000. Some people, such as farmers, spend most of their time outdoors. Others, such as storekeepers and office staff, work indoors. Schools often offer advice to help you decide which job you want to do.

DO YOU KNOW

The first industry began in Ethiopia 2 million years ago, chipping ax heads and other tools from flint stones.

Farming provides many of the basic things we need, such as fruit, vegetables, milk, meat, and wool.

Service jobs such as road-sweeping and garbage collection are important to keep the country running.

A JOB ALPHABET

How many jobs can you think of? Try making a list of jobs, starting with A for author, and ending with Z for zookeeper. You may have to make some up!

Millions of people work in factories making products, from tiny electronic devices to huge spacecraft.

Construction work employs people from all kinds of trades, such as bricklaying and plumbing.

JOB FACTS

- The biggest employer in the world is Indian Railways, with over 1.5 million people on staff.

- One of the biggest industries is car manufacturing. Every year, 7 million cars are made in Japan alone.

Lawyers and judges train for years before they are fully qualified to work in the legal profession.

Stores of all sizes sell us the goods we need. The biggest stores employ hundreds of people.

In towns and cities, many people spend most of the working day sitting at their desk in an office building.

What is the most popular food?

Rice is the world's most popular food—it is eaten in greater amounts than any other type of crop. It is mostly grown in Asian countries such as China, Japan, and India. There is a huge number of different varieties of rice—over 1,000 are grown in India alone!

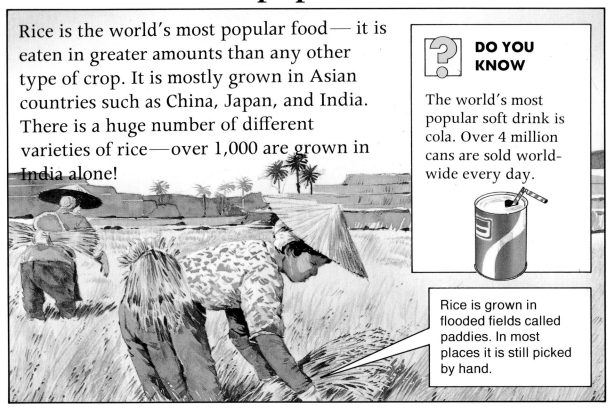

Rice is grown in flooded fields called paddies. In most places it is still picked by hand.

Who eats the most food?

People in wealthy countries eat the most food. Americans eat the most food per person, followed by Western Europeans.

The energy food gives you is measured in calories. Most people need about 2,300 calories a day, but people in poor countries often eat less than 2,000.

People in wealthy countries eat a wide range of foods. These include a lot of meat and milk products.

In poorer places, people eat fewer milk products and less meat—but more rice, fish, and vegetables.

Where are the biggest farms?

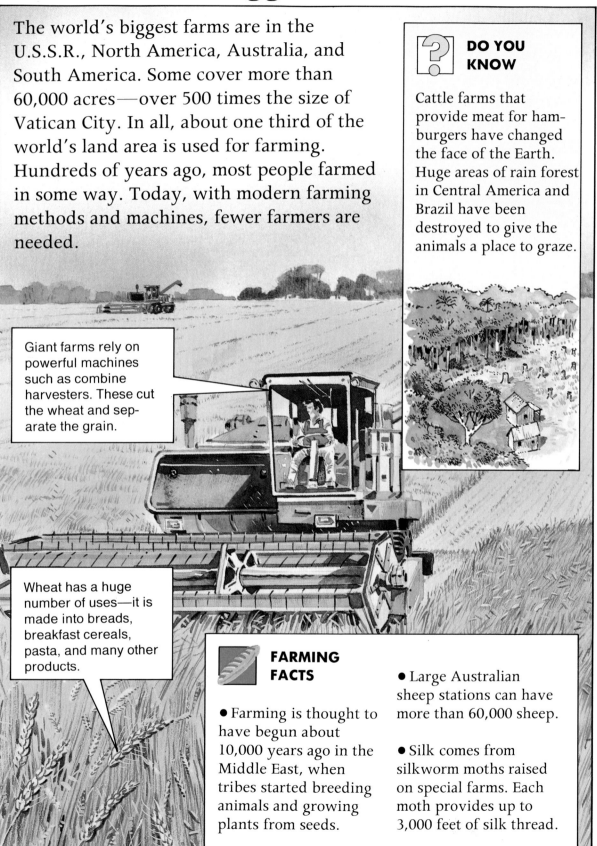

The world's biggest farms are in the U.S.S.R., North America, Australia, and South America. Some cover more than 60,000 acres—over 500 times the size of Vatican City. In all, about one third of the world's land area is used for farming. Hundreds of years ago, most people farmed in some way. Today, with modern farming methods and machines, fewer farmers are needed.

Giant farms rely on powerful machines such as combine harvesters. These cut the wheat and separate the grain.

Wheat has a huge number of uses—it is made into breads, breakfast cereals, pasta, and many other products.

? DO YOU KNOW

Cattle farms that provide meat for hamburgers have changed the face of the Earth. Huge areas of rain forest in Central America and Brazil have been destroyed to give the animals a place to graze.

FARMING FACTS

• Farming is thought to have begun about 10,000 years ago in the Middle East, when tribes started breeding animals and growing plants from seeds.

• Large Australian sheep stations can have more than 60,000 sheep.

• Silk comes from silkworm moths raised on special farms. Each moth provides up to 3,000 feet of silk thread.

Do all children go to school?

Nowadays, children in most countries have to go to school until they are teenagers. Many are able to continue their studies at colleges and universities. This is quite a recent development. Millions of people alive today have never been to school, and two-thirds of the world's population cannot read or write!

In hot places such as India, schoolchildren often have their lessons outside where there is a breeze.

Only about a third of the children in India stay on to finish their education. Most leave early to start work.

Nowadays, more than eight out of ten young Indian children go to school—far more than a few years ago.

What is the School of the Air?

Children on Australian farms often live a long way from the nearest school. That's why they join the School of the Air. They talk to their teachers by radio and send their written work by mail.

 DO YOU KNOW

In some countries it is common for children to go to boarding schools. They live at school during the term and go home for vacations. Boarders usually sleep in groups in large rooms called dormitories.

Why do some schools have uniforms?

Some schools think that uniforms help children from different backgrounds feel they all belong to the same group. School uniforms are worn in many countries, but most schools let pupils wear what they like.

 DO YOU KNOW

European gypsy children may go to several different schools in one term. Their families travel from town to town, and the children attend school wherever they happen to be.

In the Netherlands and Germany, some children live on canal barges and go to schools where the boats stop.

What are minerals?

Minerals are materials found in the ground —the word *mineral* means something that has been mined. There are about 2,500 minerals in all, including metals such as gold and silver, and gems, or precious stones, such as diamonds. Minerals have been important to us ever since our earliest ancestors used them to make flint tools.

Gold mines are the deepest mines in the world. The shaft may go down one or two miles underground.

Rubble is taken from the rock face in trucks. It is then crushed and the gold is separated from the rock.

Workers drill deep holes into the mine walls and place explosives in them to blow the rocks apart.

◆ **MINERAL FACTS**

● Over half the world's gold is mined in one area of South Africa. The deepest mines are found there, too.

● The most precious gems are diamonds, sapphires, and emeralds.

● Cut and polished diamonds only weigh about half as much as when they were found.

● Diamond is the world's hardest natural substance. It is used in industry in drill bits.

● Quartz, found in sand and rock, is the most common mineral.

What are the main fuels?

The main types of fuel are oil, natural gas, and coal. These are all fossil fuels—they were formed millions of years ago from the bodies of animals and plants—and they are all found in deposits deep underground or below the seabed.

The most important fuel is oil. Without it we'd have no gasoline, diesel oil, or kerosene. And that's not all—oil is used for plastics, medicines, and soaps as well!

The world's supply of fossil fuels will run out in about a hundred years. We'll need new sources of energy to replace them.

Scientists are now experimenting with ways to use natural energy sources that are not going to run out, such as the sun, the ocean tides, and the wind. In some places "wind farms" have already been set up. These have lots of windmill-like blades which spin around and make electricity.

In an oil well, long drills cut down to the oil deposits beneath the ocean bed. The oil is then pumped out through pipes.

Oil platforms are often sited far out to sea. Helicopters are the quickest way of bringing in workers and supplies.

Ocean oil wells have huge metal legs anchored to the seabed. The workers live on the platform high above the waves.

Why are houses so different?

Over the centuries, all kinds of houses have been built. The type of building depends on the materials available, the weather, and what purpose the house is to be used for.

In hot places, houses need to be cool inside, but in cold places they need to be as warm as possible. Some houses in Japan have paper walls to reduce damage in earthquakes, and in some rainy areas houses are built on stilts to avoid flooding.

 HOUSE FACTS

- Thousands of people are still living in caves. They are called troglodytes.

- Roman houses built 2,000 years ago often had central heating.

- Houses were lit by oil lamps and candles until about 1840.

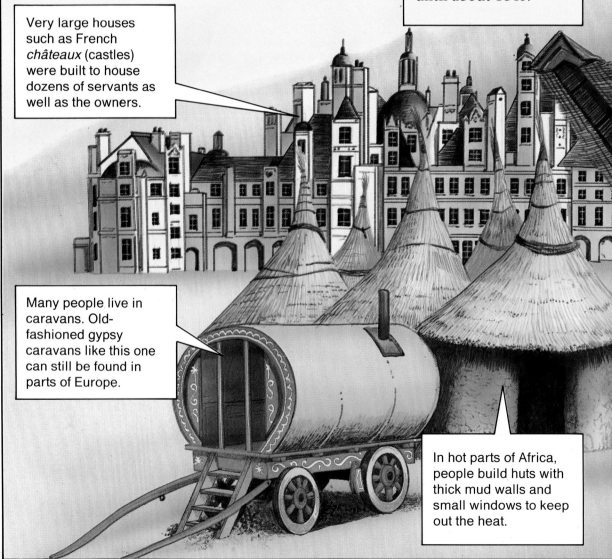

Very large houses such as French *châteaux* (castles) were built to house dozens of servants as well as the owners.

Many people live in caravans. Old-fashioned gypsy caravans like this one can still be found in parts of Europe.

In hot parts of Africa, people build huts with thick mud walls and small windows to keep out the heat.

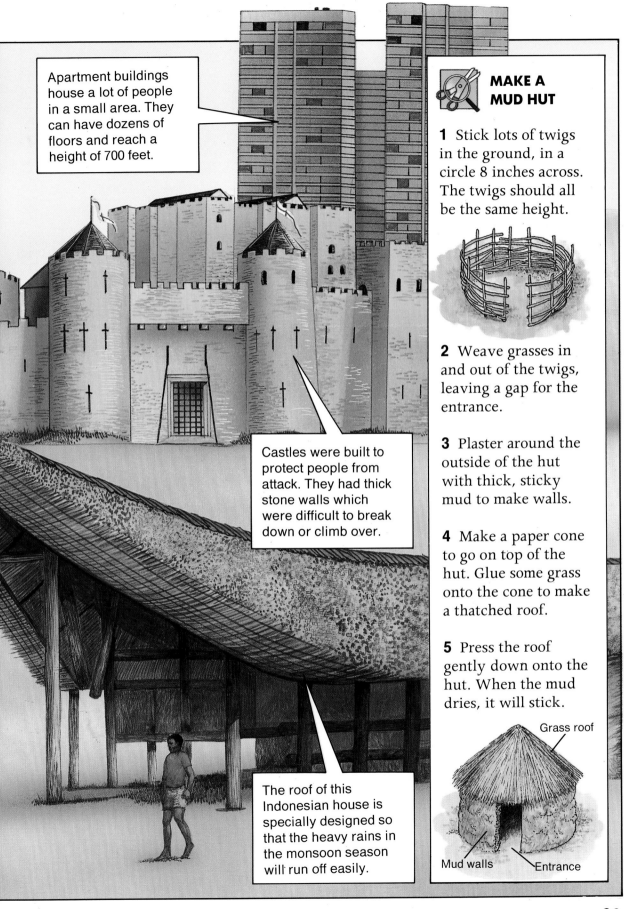

Apartment buildings house a lot of people in a small area. They can have dozens of floors and reach a height of 700 feet.

Castles were built to protect people from attack. They had thick stone walls which were difficult to break down or climb over.

The roof of this Indonesian house is specially designed so that the heavy rains in the monsoon season will run off easily.

MAKE A MUD HUT

1 Stick lots of twigs in the ground, in a circle 8 inches across. The twigs should all be the same height.

2 Weave grasses in and out of the twigs, leaving a gap for the entrance.

3 Plaster around the outside of the hut with thick, sticky mud to make walls.

4 Make a paper cone to go on top of the hut. Glue some grass onto the cone to make a thatched roof.

5 Press the roof gently down onto the hut. When the mud dries, it will stick.

Grass roof

Mud walls   Entrance

How do people live in the Sahara Desert?

The people who live in the Sahara Desert are nomads, or wanderers, who travel around in search of places where their camels and goats can graze. They belong to tribes such as the Bedouins, who often live in tents made of animal skins and goat hair.

 DO YOU KNOW

There is no furniture inside a Bedouin tent because it would be difficult to carry around. Instead there are usually cushions and rugs to sit on.

The inside of the tent may be divided into separate rooms by blankets hanging from the roof. The tent sides can be tied back to let in a cooling breeze.

How do people live in the Arctic?

Arctic people such as the Inuit once lived in tents or simple homes made from snow blocks or logs and earth. They got their food and clothing from fishing and hunting. Nowadays, though, things are different— most Inuit live in towns with modern houses and drive cars.

DO YOU KNOW

During Arctic summers the sun never sets, so it is always daylight. During midwinter the sun never rises, so it is always dark!

The traditional Inuit dog-pulled sleds have been largely replaced by snowmobiles, which have skis on the front to glide over the snow.

How do people live in the Himalayas?

The Himalayas, in Asia, form the highest mountain chain in the world. Many of the people who live in this region are shepherds who move around with their small flocks of yaks, sheep, and goats. There are few buildings other than monasteries.

DO YOU KNOW

As well as providing hair for tents and clothing, yaks supply milk to drink. Even their dung is used—as fuel for fires!

The rocky slopes of the Himalayas mean there are few roads. The main means of transportation is the yak.

How do people live in the Amazon?

The Amazon is an area of dense rain forest, where it is hot, damp, and dark. Even so, it is still home to thousands of Amazon Indians who live in villages and spend their time hunting and gathering food.

DO YOU KNOW

Some Amazon Indians use poison-tipped arrows to hunt forest animals such as monkeys. The poison comes from the tiny arrow-poison frog (below). This poison is so strong that one scratch from an arrow causes rapid death.

35

What is a city?

A city is an area where huge numbers of people live and work. There are hundreds of cities in the world, and about 80 of them have populations of over a million people.

Each country has a capital city, which is usually where the government is based.

Cities are crisscrossed with roads and railroads which link them with the outside world. Many cities are served by local airports as well.

Each city must have hospitals and schools to meet the needs of all the people living in and near the city.

The city center is filled with government buildings, offices, banks, stores, and restaurants. There are not many houses in this area.

Most city-dwellers live away from the center, in the suburbs. These are new areas of housing that have grown up around the edges of a city.

DO YOU KNOW

The oldest capital city in the world is Damascus, in Syria. People have lived there for more than 4,000 years.

One of the attractions of a city is the number of places where you can go to watch or play sports—such as football stadiums or swimming pools.

There are usually lots of places for people to visit in their spare time, such as museums, art galleries, theaters, and movie theaters.

MAKE A CITY PLAN

Some modern cities such as Brasilia in Brazil have been specially thought out by planners. Imagine you have been given the job of planning a new city. You'll need a large piece of paper or cardboard, as well as a pencil and some pens, a ruler, and an eraser.

Starting from the city center, draw in all the things you think would make your city a good place to live. Don't forget to give your city a name!

How will we live in the future?

In the years to come, new scientific developments will lead to great changes in the way we live. Computerized machines will do more of the work that people do at the moment. Space travel is certain to become more common. As our planet becomes more crowded, it is likely that people will leave Earth to live in space colonies.

DO YOU KNOW

Aircraft companies are already working to develop new space-age planes. The aim is to cut the journey time around the world from over a day to just a couple of hours!

Plans are being drawn up for a moon base, which could be a center for mining the moon's rocks.

In the future, travel by space shuttle may become as common as flying to another country is today.

Huge space stations may travel around the earth, containing colonies where people can live and work.

A SPACE-AGE HOUSE

What do you think your home will be like in 50 years' time? Design a house of the future with lots of new features. For example, it could have computer-controlled heating, lighting, and security, and robot servants to do most of the work.

Solar panels

One-way glass

Windmill

Main computer

Palm-print lock

The insides of space stations will probably be designed to be as much like Planet Earth as possible.

Useful words

Ancestor   Our ancestors are all the people who lived before us. Our earliest ancestors were the first humans, who inhabited the Earth nearly 2 million years ago.

Climate   Different parts of the world have different weather patterns. Some places are mainly hot and dry, for example, while others are mainly cold and wet. The type of weather an area has is called its climate.

Colony   A group of people who have settled together in a new place.

Drama   The general name for theatrical plays. Tragedy is a type of drama in which the stories have a sad ending.

Festival   A celebration of a special event—often with dancing, music, and feasting.

Fuel   Anything that is burned to make heat or give energy. Fossil fuels such as coal and oil were formed millions of years ago from the remains of animals and plants. Non-fossil fuels include wood, alcohol, and uranium.

General election   A general election takes place when the people of a nation elect, or choose, their government. This is done by voting—marking a piece of paper or pulling a lever to show what your choice is.

Government   The group of people who run a country. There are several forms of government, but the most common is democracy—where a new government is chosen every few years through a general election.

Industry   Work that involves the manufacture, or making, of goods. In factories, production lines pass goods from one stage of manufacturing to the next.

A car production line.

Language   The words we use to communicate with each other. Most languages can be written down, using letters or picture symbols.

Monastery   A place where religious men called monks live and work. Monasteries are often found in remote places such as high up in the mountains.

Nomads   People who wander from place to place and have no fixed home, such as desert tribes and some gypsies.

Tourist   The general word for someone who is on vacation away from home. The word *tourist* was originally used to describe someone on a tour.

Index